D is for Dazzling

Printed and bound in N. America.
Copyright ©2022 by Keisha Cuffie

All rights reserved. No part of this publication may be reproduced, stored in a retrieval system or transmitted in any form or by any means – electronic, mechanical, photocopying, and recording or otherwise – without prior written permission from the author. The exception would be brief passages by a reviewer in a newspaper or magazine or online. To perform any of the above is an infringement of copyright law. Thank you for buying an authorized copy of this book and supporting writers and their hard work.

ISBNS: 978-1-7780489-0-6 (Paperback), 978-1-7780489-4-4 (Hardcover), 978-1-7780489-1-3 (Ebook).
First Edition: February 2022

Written and designed by: Keisha Cuffie
Illustrations by: Hameo Pham

"To my beautiful Dazzling Stars, you are the reasons I continue to fight for equality in this world."

D IS FOR DAZZLING

Do you know that you are like a shimmering star in the night sky? Each one, original and unique!

I'll tell you a secret that you should always remember...

There is no one else like you in the whole universe! Do you know what that means?

That you are the most incredible, simply sensational, only one of you!

You are amazing, for all the stories you tell that light up the world!

You are generous, for all the hugs and kisses you give to those you love.

You are kind, for all the time you take to show people that you care.

You are beautiful, for all the joy your smile brings when it lights up your face.

You are happy, for all the giggles you make when you get your tickles!

You are strong, for all the times you get up when you fall down.

You are brilliant because you never stop trying even when things are difficult.

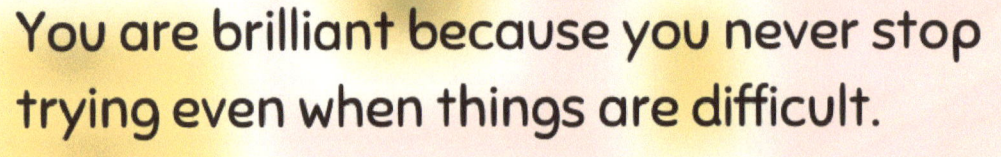

You are determined because you practice to be the best you can be!

You are insightful because you know it's okay to experience all your emotions!

You are powerful because your voice and what you have to say matters!

So, now you know why we say D is for Dazzling...

The only one of you in the whole universe!

ABOUT THE AUTHOR

As an Early Childhood Professional, Ms. Keisha saw few inclusive diverse children's books written by Canadian authors in classrooms, libraries and early childhood settings. Aiming to change this, she wrote 'D is for Dazzling' to showcase diversity, inclusion and empowerment while providing children with books featuring positive affirmations. Representation Matters.

As a person who is passionate about sharing Black Canadian History, under the pen name CurlyKeish, her motto is: "Education is only complete, when it includes all the shared experiences of our joint histories."

D is for Dazzling is the first in a series of books on empowerment written by this up and coming Canadian author.

CPSIA information can be obtained
at www.ICGtesting.com
Printed in the USA
BVHW020354290922
648251BV00001B/6